BIRD NESTS

TEXT BY
SHARON A. COHEN

PRINCIPAL PHOTOGRAPHY BY
GERRY ELLIS

CollinsPublishersSanFrancisco
A Division of HarperCollins*Publishers*

First published 1993 by
Collins Publishers San Francisco, 1160 Battery Street
San Francisco, California 94111

Produced by Welcome Enterprises, Inc.
164 East 95th Street, New York, New York 10128
Designer: Nai Chang
Project Manager: Hiro Clark
Editor: Ellen Mendlow

Compilation copyright © 1993 Welcome Enterprises, Inc.
Text copyright © 1993 Sharon A. Cohen
Gerry Ellis photographs copyright © 1993 Gerry Ellis
All rights reserved, including the right of reproduction
in whole or in part in any form.

Library of Congress Cataloging-in-Publication Data

Cohen, Sharon (Sharon Anne)
    Bird Nests / text by Sharon A. Cohen ; principal pho-
  tography by Gerry Ellis.
      p. cm.
    Includes index.
ISBN 0-00-255110-1
1. Birds--Nests. 2. Birds--Nests--Pictorial works.   I. Ellis,
Gerry.   II. Title.
QL675.C63 1993
598.2' 564--dc20   92-44031
                                      CIP

Printed in Singapore by Tien Wah Press
2 4 6 8 10 9 7 5 3 1

Page 1: Rufous Hummingbird
Page 2: Gentoo Penguins

CONTENTS

Mourning Dove Nest and Eggs

INTRODUCTION

Birds are popularly considered the harbingers of spring. During that season, hardly a day goes by without a chorus of whistles, songs, screeches, and rat-a-tats, a bright beaming or flashing of color, an undulating flight pattern, or a tender exchange of affection among our avian friends.

For most birds, springtime means mating, and mating time means nesting. As soon as nesting begins in earnest, everything changes. The earth becomes quieter, the sight of a bird rarer. Despite the seeming tranquility, there's still much ado and excitement among the birds. The joy of expressing the springtime, of finding or reclaiming a mate, has been exchanged for the silence and secrecy of very private moments as birds begin the work of creating their homes.

Herring Gull Chicks Hatching

A hummingbird hovers over a spider's web, spending several seconds latching onto a thread of silk. A woodpecker suspends his tree-drumming and instead works on excavating a nest hole with his mate. A shorebird slinks into a quiet area unnoticed and lays her single egg on bare sand. In the privacy of their own world, often far beyond human ken, birds settle down to build their nests and breed young.

After mating takes place, attracting attention is no longer a priority. Instead it is protecting the nest and incubating eggs that matter. All living beings are driven to reproduce, and most lay eggs. What makes birds different from other egg-laying creatures is that the embryo inside each egg is as warm-blooded as a human, and like a human, requires the warmth provided by its parent, or by an adequate substitute, to develop and to thrive. Because it is so fragile, the egg must be coddled in a secure place until its occupant is ready to leave and face the rigors of the outside world. Encased in its shell, the tiny chick's only hope is that its parents do know what is best. The nest the adult birds provide furnishes the warmth and protection necessary for their chicks' survival.

It would be nice to say that once nests are built, eggs laid, and birds settled down to brood, a truce of sorts is called in the animal kingdom. Unfortunately for nesting birds, nothing is further from the truth. Many reptiles, mammals, and even other birds salivate at egg-laying time. A sedentary bird and its vulnerable eggs make particularly appealing prey.

Common Iora and Chicks

When a bird, in most cases a natural flier, has to spend hours, days, or sometimes months in its nest incubating eggs, it enters into one of the most difficult periods of its life. It must combat its natural inclination to flee in the face of danger in favor of protecting its eggs. In many cases, there is little choice but to abandon the nest. Eggs could be destroyed while the parent is out searching for food; or a predator might threaten the adult's life sufficiently to make remaining at the nest a foolhardy idea, endangering both adult and chick.

Adults scare easily from the nest when their young are still encased inside their fragile shells, but this soon changes after the chicks are hatched. With helpless lives now before it, the parent bird's commitment increases greatly, and it is prepared to fight, sometimes even to the death, to defend its charges.

With chicks present, activity begins to return to the breeding grounds. High-pitched chirps and squeals of never-satisfied, hungry youngsters replace the billing and cooing of wooing mates. In some cases, the nestlings are blind and featherless and remain clinging to the safety of the nest. In others, the chicks are miniature versions of their parents who will soon leave the nest to seek food on their own.

Most remain close to the nest until they are fledged. Fledging is the avian equivalent of graduation, but instead of a diploma, a bird gets its wings; it is old enough to leave the nest and the security it represents. In a few cases, the youngsters stay nearby, and even help their parents rear the next batch of nestlings. Most times, however, the young birds fly off, seemingly anxious to court and build nests of their own. The empty nest that they leave behind them serves as the sole memento of the connection between parent and young—a moment as fleeting and brief as the springtime.

Black-headed Heron Fledglings

9

PART ONE

Love on the Wing

I n the avian world, foreplay lasts much longer than sex. While the actual act of insemination takes place in a matter of seconds, courtship rituals can occupy days or even weeks. This slow process of bonding has a definite purpose: it not only establishes connections, it engenders trust in normally solitary birds.

Finding a mate can be as complicated for birds as for humans. In fact, birds have to contend with one difficulty people don't often face: it isn't always easy to determine just by looking the difference between male and female. In many bird species, the distinction is clear: the male is larger or more brightly colored, the female smaller and drab. But in others, the sexes are virtually indistinguishable. (Birders are not alone. Even warblers have trouble telling themselves apart.)

PRECEDING PAGES: *The Common Peafowl* (Pavo cristatus), *popularly known as the peacock, shows off its fanned colorful tail in one of the most remarkable displays in the bird kingdom. Originally a native of India and nearby regions, the peacock has been introduced throughout the world.*

LEFT*: The male Gambel's Quail* (Lophortyx gambelii) *is more lavishly colored than the female.*

OPPOSITE: *Black Terns* (Chlidonias niger) *use fish to lure their mates. Sometimes one male is tricked by another pretending to be female just to get a free meal.*

Performing a courtship ritual is a polite way for one bird to find out if it is pursuing the right partner. In addition to sexual identification there are the problems of species recognition and sexual readiness. All these issues are raised and addressed during the courtship process. Birds give visual and vocal cues that convey their intended messages clearly to rivals and prospective partners. Not every such signal will be met with ready acceptance and glee, however; often one bird's advance is met with aggression instead of welcome, particularly when a less experienced, younger male dares to trespass on another male's territory.

Rituals begun for courting purposes also serve to ensure good parental cooperation. Even pairs that successfully bred in seasons past benefit from time spent renewing their relationship. In most bird species fathers play an involved, active role in reproductive efforts with one female, though some bird species are in fact polygamous. Polygamous birds rely on the odds being in their favor: with more nests in use, they are more likely to pass on their genes.

Few other creatures in the animal kingdom practice this endeavor with so much variety and seeming intensity. Bird courtship embraces avian versions of gift-giving, serenades, dancing, and self-conscious romantic settings, all in prelude to nesting and raising chicks. Courtship rituals, though ostensibly unfair to the less gifted, ensure that only the most visual, vocal, or creative bird will leave its genetic legacy to future generations.

TENDER INTERACTIONS

In many cases, birds prefer their solitude. Rather than longing for the company of friends, they learn to fear other birds, even those of their own kind. This behavior becomes a problem when it comes time to mate. A loner must learn some social skills in a hurry.

Courtship rituals ease the naturally existing tensions of otherwise solitary birds. The process is something akin to prolonged dating before even the first kiss is exchanged. The pair must get over their fears and aggressive tendencies.

Couples smooth frictions through a gradual sequence that may involve the passing of food, the singing of song, or a series of displays. For some birds, such as parrots, herons, pigeons, and crows, one of the final stages of this get-acquainted process, aside from actual copulation, is a tender physical interaction, a mutual grooming session called allopreening.

In the lowland forests of Papua New Guinea, Black-capped Lory males spread their wings and cock their heads to the side. In this awkward position, they bounce up and down, while staying focused on a particular female of their choice. One male's actions are rewarded when a hen approaches and begins to pick at the lice embedded in his neck feathers. This gesture is much appreciated by the love-struck male, who can't quite reach this spot with his own hooked beak, and he demonstrates his gratitude by repaying the favor. Their little engagement has just inaugurated a lifelong partnership.

A Black-capped Lory female (Lorius lory) grooms her mate. Black-capped Lories dwell in Papua New Guinea and offshore islands.

Although South America's Military Macaws (Ara militaris) and most other macaws mate for life, the couples must constantly assure each other and reinforce their bond through mutual feeding and preening. Before copulation, many males ritually knead their partners' backs; they jump aboard and seemingly walk in place. How this prepares them for mating is not generally understood but perhaps it serves as a gentle massage.

Trumpeter Swans (Cygnus buccinator) *inhabit refuges in the northwestern United States and parts of Canada. To chase off territorial intruders, pairs raise and flap their wings while extending their necks. If this doesn't work, they follow up with feather-pulling and aerial pursuits. After successfully defending their territory, pairs celebrate by swimming toward each other with necks lowered and wings trailing behind.*

LOVE SONGS

For songbirds and other bird groups, song plays a key role in the courtship process. The gift of song is primarily a male phenomenon, though many females do sing, sometimes in so close a duet with their male partners that it is difficult to separate the two voices. A female chooses her mate primarily for the excellence of his performance, though what to her ears sounds beautiful may be mere noise to us. Indeed, for those bird species without the range or ability to perform an avian aria, a clamorous noise is the next best thing. Yet no matter what the resultant sound, it's music to a female's ears.

The mating song of the Red-winged Blackbird varies, depending on whether he is at rest or in flight. It is usually accompanied by some type of wing movement, enough for a glimpse of his crimson shoulder patches or a full flashing when the song is at its most intense. Even with his bright red shoulder epaulets barely in sight, this marsh-dwelling bird has no intention of going unnoticed. With head tilted high, he belts out a long and complex song. It is usually the grand finale, a vibrating trill, and not the complicated prelude, that lures possible mates. His has already sparked the interest of one female (now nesting), and he is hoping to succeed in attracting more than one mate to his territory this year. When an intruding male enters his domain, the song becomes more vigorous—enough to convince the errant male to retreat as quickly as he appeared.

The Red-winged Blackbird (Agelaius phoeniceus) *makes its home in North and Central America.*

Australia's Laughing Kookaburra (Dacelo gigas) is not blessed with a melodious song, but its raucous laughter certainly commands attention. Pairs call out to their neighbors in early morning outbursts, announcing their territorial claims to all.

LEFT: *Found on the east coast of the United States, Boat-tailed Grackles* (Quiscalus major) *attend mass sing-alongs to begin their courting. Once joined, the newfound couples engage in duets of hoarse whistles to proclaim their bond for all to hear.*

OPPOSITE: *Yellow-headed Blackbirds*(Xanthoceph-alus xanthocephalus) *of western North America croak out their strangled notes, often in the company of fellow males. Considering the lustiness with which they belt out their tunes, it is quite apparent they have no idea they can't sing.*

20

Instead of singing, the woodpecker taps out his message to females who find the sound as irresistible as Orpheus' lyre. Once a pair meets, a more harmonic call sounded by both members replaces the tree-drumming. The female lets out an ecstatic cry to declare her readiness to mate, and her partner willingly obliges her. Hairy Woodpeckers (Picoides villosus) make their homes throughout most of North America.

*Unlike their cousins in the woodpecker family, flickers are often found where they feed—at ground level. In addition to tree-drumming, flickers and woodpeckers rely on a series of calls, either to notify their lifelong mates that they have arrived at the breeding grounds, or to define their territory for neighboring males. Yellow-shafted Flickers (*Colaptes auratus*) are the eastern variation of the Common Flicker, found throughout North America.*

COURTING COLORS

During breeding season, when appearances really do count, many males are transformed into vain show-offs. Some are blessed with stunning beauty year-round, while others don crests and colorful patterns only seasonally. But no matter the duration, the intent is universal: be noticed! Camouflage may be the optimum defense against attack, but when reproductive concerns supersede survival tactics, the best often equals the brightest—and most colorful. Many females choose their mates on the basis of presentation alone.

Surely there is no better example of visual splendor than that displayed by many members of the bird of paradise family. High atop a private staging area in the thick moist forests of Australia and Papua New Guinea, the males show off their particular specialties: twisted wires, long luxuriant plumes, and fans that could steal the attention away from a flamenco dancer. The females select the finest males for mating, thus continuing the genetic lines of only the most ornately gifted males. Many female admirers are so impressed by some offerings that they choose their mates from species within the bird of paradise family other than their own. Since the aim of these promiscuous birds is to impregnate as many females as possible, the males are only too pleased to oblige interested females of all stripes. Interbreeding, while rare for most birds, is common among birds of paradise.

LEFT AND OPPOSITE:
Male birds of paradise usually have to wait eight or nine years before their plumage reaches its full, competitive potential. Once they do seize the spotlight, they take maximum advantage. The Raggiana Bird of Paradise (Paradisaea raggiana) has been known to turn upside down in an effort to stress its long, luxuriant tail plumes, while other birds of paradise tear down overhanging leaves to allow the sun to glow on their iridescent plumage. The Raggiana Bird of Paradise lives in the rain forests of Papua New Guinea.

Willow Ptarmigan (Lagopus lagopus), found in northern Canada and Alaska, change colors seasonally, from white in winter to reddish brown in the summer. Breeding males retain some markings that counteract their camouflage and assure that they are still attractive to females. They retain the white plumage on their bottom halves and acquire defined bright red arches over their eyes. Later in the season, they molt to a more discreet brown with only a touch of white.

26

Tufted Puffins (Fratercula cirrhata) *live in and near the Pacific coastal waters of North America. During breeding season, the normally drab appearance of the male changes dramatically. The completely black head and orange bill are transformed into a mostly white face with an orange- and lemon-colored bill, complemented by long streaming yellowish tufts of hair that begin at the rear of their eyes and extend gracefully to their backs.*

*Magnificent Frigatebirds
(Fregata magnificens)
are found on both the
Atlantic and Pacific coasts
of tropical America.*

FLASHING BEACONS

The commotion caused when a male Magnificent Frigatebird lands on a coastal tree with a large twig in his beak is amplified by many indignant squawks as other frigatebird males protest the disturbance of their nest-building process. After several days of gathering materials, the waiting period has begun for most, interrupted only by short fishing forays.

The male birds sit expectantly on their makeshift nests and gaze at the sky. It is not long before their patience is rewarded by a female flying overhead. Head back, bill in the air, each inflates his red gular patch as a child would blow a balloon—to just before the bursting point. Caught up in the competition, some drum their hooked beaks onto the distention in hopes of attracting atten-tion. For one lucky male, the ploy works, and the female lands beside him

OPPOSITE: *Africa's White-cheeked Turacos* (Tauraco leucotis) *are known for their unique green pigmentation as well as red flashes of color on their flight feathers. But color plays no part in courtship. Instead, males present regurgitated fruit pulp to their mates.*

RIGHT: *When males and females look alike and color changes are not an option, birds must use other means of getting a partner's attention. Male Spinifex Pigeons* (Petrophassa plumifera) *of Australia perform bowing displays, lowering their heads to the ground and spreading their tail feathers to flash their hindquarters at prospective mates.*

in acquisition. After her egg is laid, the male's pouch fades from bright crimson to a pale orange.

While many birds go through abrupt color changes during breeding season, others, such as Magnificent Frigatebirds, have the ability to flash a bright color year-round. These birds need to be inconspicuous to avoid the ongoing threat of predators, but must also have a colorful lure to attract mating females. Temporary color bursts that last until a partnership is established are the perfect compromise.

ON DISPLAY

RIGHT AND OPPOSITE: *Sage Grouse* (Centrocercus urophasianus) *gather at leks on the western plains of the United States.*

Male grouse, quail, and other fowl-like birds routinely gather at traditional display grounds called leks—flat, open spaces the size of suburban backyards—to advertise their wares. A haphazard gathering of Sage Grouse on a grassy plain seems at first to lack organization, but at the center of this congregation stands the largest and most colorful bird of all. Just as humans may inflate their lungs, the dominant male Sage Grouse enlarges his external breast sacs to their maximum by taking an exhaustively deep

Though it isn't always apparent, each grouse has his own territory, sometimes encompassing only a few yards. Battle for prime spots involves much wing-slapping, but rarely results in harm to either bird. Achieving the coveted central position has ample rewards. The central male gets to mate with most of the breeding females and, insulated by surrounding males, he is the least likely to be attacked should a predator approach.

breath. When the Sage Grouse exhales, a vacant, plopping sound reverberates throughout the area.

Like discriminating shoppers searching for a bargain, the hens watch the males' display in appreciation until they spot the best deal—usually the dominant male at the center. This system rewards nearly all admiring females; each takes her turn, preferably with the dominant male, but will also accept advances from subordinate males.

Though only a few of the thirty-odd males have the opportunity to mate, the others learn much from watching their superiors—how to strut, drum their wings, fan their tails, and fight for prime territory within the lek. Next year, it may be one of these birds that the females line up to see.

Found in the grasslands and sagebrush of the northern United States and Canada, Sharp-tailed Grouse (Tympanuchus phasianellus) lift their tail feathers to flash their rumps and inflate their purple neck-pouches during courtship displays. Song, cacklings, and soft cooings make an important accompaniment to their pageantry.

BELOW: *The Great Bowerbird* (Chlamydera nuchalis) *builds the largest avenue bower. The arched walls stand as high as eighteen inches and up to four feet long.*

OPPOSITE TOP: *Using a piece of woodpulp drenched in a mixture of charcoal and saliva,* Satin Bowerbirds (Ptilono-rhynchus violaceus) *paint their bower interiors black. Blue objects adorn both the inside and outside of the bower.*

OPPOSITE BOTTOM: *Australia's Golden Bowerbird* (Prionodura newtoniana) *makes his bower in a maypole style, with columns of sticks built around small trees. At up to nine feet tall, it is the tallest bower built.*

ARCHITECTURAL ALLURE

In heavily forested areas, such as those of Papua New Guinea and Australia, there is little room for a courting bird to show off. While promiscuous birds of paradise get around this by flaunting adornments and other attention-grabbers, their less conspicuous cousins, the bowerbirds, have to employ more creative means to woo their mates.

Though some bowerbirds are colorful, most are drab and would have a difficult time making an impression on appearances alone. Instead, bowerbirds resort to one of the most creative courtship methods in the bird world—if you can't impress them with your looks, affect them with your talents. In a masterful display of architectural prowess, male bowerbirds construct simple or complex archways that serve the same function as the showy appendages of their more colorful compatriots: calling attention to themselves and advertising their availability.

Each bower has a distinctive look, depending on the species. Generally, the more somberly colored the builder, the more ornate the bower. Building materials usually consist of branches, accented with whatever suits the designer's fancy. A Great Bowerbird's courtship bower encloses a pathway strewn with white rocks and shells, while a Satin Bowerbird surrounds his with blue objects. After a complex display, the best artisans are rewarded by visiting females. Ironically, more work and skill goes into building the courting bower than into the simple cup nest females use to raise the chicks.

PAS DE DEUX

A grebe walking on land is one of the most comical sights in the natural world. He takes two steps. He falls flat on his face on the third. He picks himself up and walks four more steps and then plop! he's down again.

Despite their awkwardness on land, grebes and many other long-necked birds, such as cranes and flamingos, are at their most graceful and coordinated when performing their mating dances—just as long as they are in their proper element. For grebes, whose rudderlike feet are positioned at their tails instead of near their gravitational centers, a smooth-surfaced lake makes the ideal stage for a balletic pas de deux. A male and female pair glide smoothly across the water, with necks arched, and feet paddling in frenetic S curves, in near-perfect unison.

For some grebes, the dance is the final act in a series of rituals: a haunting sequence of calls to re-establish old bonds or form new ones, followed by display postures or presentations of long stringy weeds.

The synchronized movements of courting grebes and other bird species help the couple determine the right time to copulate. The cooperation forged during the dance also cements their bond and makes raising a family all the easier.

Western Grebes (Aechmophorus occidentalis) *inhabit inland waters of western North and Central America.*

The courtship of cranes has inspired the dances of traditional peoples worldwide. Their elaborate duets include leaps, undulations, and perfectly matched motions. Africa's Black-crowned Cranes (Balearica regulorum) synchronize their body cycles and develop bonds through dance. Even the youngest cranes practice dancing as a means of appeasement when anxious or threatened. Established pairs, whose bonds are already assured, often dispense with dancing altogether.

PART TWO

The Well-Built Nest

Birds build nests as varied as human homes—creating their own versions of huts, adobes, townhouses, apartment buildings, and castles. Restricted to what is available in nature's hardware store, birds spend hours, weeks, or even months in the building process. The variety and frequent complexity of nests are astonishing in light of the fact that birds work only with tools that nature has provided; using their beaks, their claws, and sometimes their backs, birds carry materials, excavate holes, and sew or weave.

Almost anything light enough for a bird to carry can become part of a nest, including man-made items such as ribbons, plastic, and string. The principal natural sources include the three major categories of the earth: animal, vegetable, and mineral. Plant matter, from bulky tree branches to soft lichen, ranks as the most popular ingredient, as it is readily available and easily manipulated.

PREVIOUS PAGES:
A colony of Masked Weavers (Ploceus intermedius) *take over an African Acacia tree.*

LEFT AND OPPOSITE:
Two Masked Weavers build quite different-looking nests. Location and available materials very much determine what each bird creates.

Instinct drives the building process and experience teaches that certain steps must be followed to avoid failure. Yet even when birds do observe procedure, success is far from guaranteed. Some intangibles, such as weather, predation, and humans, are impossible to predict. A shortage of space or food can lead birds to curtail or postpone their nesting completely. Under such difficult circumstances some birds will even usurp another's nest.

The location of a nest can easily determine success or failure in reproducing. The chosen site must be secure from predators, able to support a growing brood, protected from the elements, and close to a food source.

Linking a particular nest with the species of bird that built it can prove diffi-

cult. Nests of different species that share the same habitat sometimes look almost identical. Logic may help narrow the choices. A chick that can fend for itself shortly after hatching will want a nest it can easily escape, while one that needs more parental care will require a solid structure that can hold and protect its body while it is still a developing chick.

The singularity of each individual nest results from a chance combination of factors including the builder's experience, materials at hand, habitat, and most important of all, the type of bird. Yet, one common thread binds all the diversity of nests. Whether massive or tiny, complicated or simple in structure, a nest is that which bears and protects the egg.

IN A SCRAPE

An Arctic Tern protects its eggs. Arctic Terns (Sterna paradisaea) *are found in Europe, Asia, and North and South America.*

Though the popular image of a nest is an elaborate construction of twigs, straw, and feathers, the scrape nest is a much simpler affair. A bird builds a scrape much the way people make snow angels. By pressing closely to the ground while rotating on sandy or other easily modified surfaces, the bird forms a shallow depression. Backward kicking action aids the process.

The first scrapes may have come about by accident—the result of courting birds circling each other or vying for position. Birds that added adornments to the primitive site began the architectural evolution into more complicated nest types.

These slight depressions are meant to take up the smallest space possible. Scrapes are usually found in open areas with little or no cover. To compensate for the lack of protection, birds nesting in scrapes typically do so in large colonies, often in remote locations such as islands where there are few predators.

The bird nesting in a scrape has much to do to look after its eggs. Without cozy, supportive sides to protect them, eggs do not stay warm without almost constant attention from a parent. Also, they roll out of the shallow nest easily. Arctic Terns grab onto errant eggs with hooked bills, slowly pulling them back toward the nest. Since eggs refuse to roll in a consistent direction, accomplishing this can be no small feat.

One of the advantages of a scrape is that it takes so little time to build. This is particularly helpful to the Arctic Tern, whose 20,000-mile round-trip trek is the longest recorded migration route. Since the Arctic summer is so brief, a simple scrape that does not shorten brooding time is the best solution.

A Red-tailed Tropicbird
(Phaethon rubricauda) *sits*
in its scrape. Red-tailed
Tropicbirds nest on Australian
cliffs and shores.

Some birds, such as American Oystercatchers (Haematopus palliatus), *found on the tropical coasts of North and South America, add little if any embellishment to their scrapes. A typical oystercatcher nest holds two or three eggs.*

Though the Western Gull (Larus occidentalis) *makes its scrape with only a minimal amount of grass, it often repairs and uses the same nest in successive seasons. The Western Gull is the only gull to nest on the coast of California. Its breeding range extends throughout the Pacific Coast of North America.*

A BURROWING ANIMAL

Once a flock of Southern Carmine Bee-eaters has finished building nesting burrows, the sloping sides of an African riverbed resemble Swiss cheese. Dozens of colorful birds flutter to and from tiny entranceways. Fragile riverbanks sometimes cave in when they cannot withstand the onslaught.

Although burrowing is not one of the many talents for which birds are famous, many species are actually quite accomplished diggers. Why a creature that could fly to safer territory would choose to nest in the ground remains a mystery, especially since nests are so easily raided by snakes and other hunters. Scientists believe that burrows are essentially expanded scrapes, with the added protection of concealment.

Bee-eaters begin building their burrows by flying directly into riverbanks—an experience roughly akin to running headlong into a plasterboard wall trying to make a dent. Often after several knocks on the head, a temporary landing forms, from which the bird can begin shoveling dirt backward. The bird must be quick and efficient in its movements; once it has begun, the bee-eater cannot retreat until it builds the terminal nesting chamber and has room to turn around.

Bee-eaters line their nesting chambers with regurgitated insect parts, whose aroma in no way compares to the stink left behind by fish remains casually discarded in kingfisher tunnels. Unsavory as this may sound, the refuse serves as a deterrent to intruders who might wish to investigate. Other birds, such as Burrowing Owls, use similar methods to repel predators.

PRECEDING PAGES: *Southern Carmine Bee-eaters* (Merops nubicoides) *nest in large flocks in southern Africa.*

RIGHT: *Breeding on the northwest coast of North America, Horned Puffins* (Fratercula corniculata) *nest in well-concealed holes along cliff faces. Males and females dig their burrows with both feet and bills. In the absence of available burrowing space, they lay their eggs in rock crevices or under bushes.*

Nesting inside deep burrows along the southern coasts of South America, Magellanic Penguins (Spheniscus magellanicus) *pile sticks, pebbles, and leaves into mounds up to ten feet high. Eggs laid on a feather bed at the top of these tall piles stay dry as rainwater accumulates at the bottom of the subterranean burrows.*

HIDDEN HAUNTS

For secrecy, few hiding places can compare to a tree cavity. Except to those lucky enough to stumble upon one, they are virtually undetectable. Usually, the foliage of surrounding trees provides ample camouflage; sometimes height is the great advantage. No matter the case, birds nesting in tree cavities are safe from most predators—except for tree-climbing snakes and an occasional agile mammal.

A tree must be large and structurally sound enough to support a cavity, especially when carved by the Pileated Woodpecker. The Pileated digs a hollow up to two feet into the tree, although the 3½-inch entranceway is only a fraction that size. The Pileated Woodpecker is equipped with one of the strongest beaks of all birds, yet excavating comes as no easy chore. The process takes days, and is completed mostly by the male with some assistance from his mate. Many choose dead trees, but even so their efforts may be frustrated by a particularly recalcitrant tree.

Not every cavity nester possesses a bill strong enough to dig his own. Owls, parrots, and Wood Ducks all depend on other birds' abandoned nests for their breeding sites. Relying on the handiwork of the Pileated Woodpecker in such cases can have its drawbacks. Though these birds don't add dung to their entrances, their own wastes are not routinely removed. Even dead chicks may be left in the chamber if they are too heavy to move. Pileateds devote their energies to laying eggs and digging holes, leaving any cleanup duties to future tenants.

Pileated Woodpeckers (Dryocopus pileatus) *are found throughout the eastern United States and Canada.*

Boreal Owls (Aegolius funereus) inhabit thick forests of the northern United States, Canada, and Alaska. Most owls do not build their own nests. Rather, they expropriate abandoned nesting cavities, often woodpecker holes. Larger owls tend to nest in old hawk or crow nests, especially when they cannot locate cavities large enough for their needs.

BELOW: *Found throughout most of North America, nocturnal Northern Saw-whet Owls* (Aegolius acadicus) *spend most of their daylight hours in or near their nesting cavities.*

ABOVE: *The smallest North American owl, at six inches in height, the Flammulated Owl* (Otus flammeolus) *requires only a small hollow to nest in.*

57

LEFT: *Until a female arrives and selects a cavity for nesting, a male House Wren* (Troglodytes aedon) *of North America may claim and clean out up to seven tree cavities, including those belonging to his neighbors. Though the male may make rudimentary beginnings to the nest, the female adds the finishing touches. House Wrens also inhabit the West Indies and Central and South America.*

OPPOSITE: *The recesses of a hollow tree provide limited room for a growing merganser family, which might include ten or eleven hungry chicks. When two families share the same nest, space can be even tighter. Common Mergansers* (Mergus merganser) *live in North America and Europe.*

LOFTY DESIGNS

The Florida Everglades are the winter home to a myriad of bird species. Landing atop one of the highest trees in the area, a pair of Ospreys join the residents. Both were born nearby and though neither can recognize a specific home nest, they know the territory is familiar.

The male bird alighting on a dead tree branch brings it crashing to the ground. The Osprey swoops, then rises, bearing in his talons the first piece of his nest, a platform made up of long, thick branches. Both birds repeat the process many times, sometimes catching the branch in midair. After a week, the nest is complete, but instead of mating, the pair fly off.

There isn't anything wrong with the nest they built. In fact, it is a perfect aerie for an Osprey. High atop a tree with visibility on all sides, it is within a few miles of an excellent fishing spot. At this altitude, their offspring should be safe from most danger. This year, however, there will be no egg-laying. These two are only in their second year of life and are still incapable of mating.

Ospreys are among the few birds who build nests a year before they inhabit them. The pair will most likely return the following season to use the nest they built, lining it with leaves and feathers for breeding. In most cases, the same Osprey duo adds to the nest in succeeding years, creating a structure of gigantic proportions—perhaps five feet in diameter and seven high. Their home might even play host to some freeloading House Sparrows or grackles, who are known to borrow a corner of the Ospreys' residence for their own nesting needs.

ABOVE AND OPPOSITE: *Ospreys* (Pandion haliaetus) *can be found in nearly any part of the world, except for the polar regions and South America. The Osprey at right adds another branch to its aerie.*

The Bald Eagle
(Haliaeetus leuco-
cephalus) *uses a plat-*
form nest as its base
and then builds a
more complicated cup
nest into the surface.
If disturbed during
egg-laying or early
chick-rearing, a Bald
Eagle pair may aban-
don its nest.

Bald Eagles sometimes add to their aeries for twenty years or more, and nests have been known to approach two tons. Bald Eagles can be found in North America.

Ferruginous Hawks (Buteo regalis) *build aeries in much of the western half of the United States. Depending on the available food supply, they lay three to five eggs each season.*

AN ARBOREAL DEMITASSE

Rufous Hummingbirds (Selasphorus rufus) *are found in northwestern North America.*

Even the most careful observer would be challenged to locate a hummingbird's nest. This smallest of nests is nearly impossible to find, not only because of its size, but as a result of the plant camouflage the female incorporates into the structure.

Because of the importance of camouflage, males are not welcome visitors to the hummingbird nest. Their bright colors draw too much attention and might endanger the offspring, so they take no part in nest-building, incubation, or chick-rearing. Often they return after the chicks are fledged and help produce a second brood in the same season.

For hummingbird chicks, which must remain in the nest until their feathers have grown and they are able to fend for themselves, a cup is the ideal nest. The supportive sides of a cup prevent the nestlings from tumbling out, and the cup-shaped structure keeps them warm when their parents are away. Most nests are built starting at the base, by entwining materials around a thin branch until a ball is formed. While the bird is standing on the top of the ball, the sides are pulled up, added to, and then camouflaged. The hummingbird constructs her nest from the most delicate natural fibers she can find. The structure of spiderwebs, lichen, and mosses is expandable; as the chicks grow, so grows the nest.

Not every bird could manage a cup nest. Because of the high walls, a cup must be entered from above, a feat best accomplished by skilled aviators such as songbirds. Master of wing control, the hummingbird is a natural cup nester.

LEFT: *Chicks rest snugly inside this Magnolia Warbler* (Dendroica magnolia) *nest. Found in coniferous forests of the northern United States and Canada, and wintering as far south as the West Indies, Magnolia Warblers build nests that blend readily into the trees.*

OPPOSITE: *At two feet wide and nearly a foot high, the American Crow's* (Corvus brachyrynchos) *nest is one of the largest cup nests. It takes a pair of crows about two weeks to build and usually supports four to six hungry nestlings. Young crows, possibly from last year's brood, remain near their parents' nest. Some observers believe these youngsters play a part in territorial defense or feeding the new brood of chicks.*

BLOWING IN THE WIND

Oriole nests are North America's closest relation to the oropendola nests of South America. Averaging six inches in length, the Northern Oriole's (Icterus galbula) nest is smaller, but nearly as intricate.

Cup nests serve the crucial function of encasing eggs and chicks in a cozy sanctuary, but they provide little refuge from tree-climbing mammals and snakes. One solution is to situate the nest so that it is safe from creatures that can climb. By suspending a cup from the branch of a tree, beyond easy reach, a bird reaps the benefits of the cup while affording some additional protection to its young. Such nests are known as hanging or pensile nests.

A variation on the pensile nest is the pendulous nest, the most impressive of which belong to the oropendolas of South America. The three- or four-foot-long nests of interwoven grasses resemble Christmas stockings and can sometimes hang twenty to thirty feet off the ground.

Oropendolas enter their nests from the top, but lay their eggs in a simple cup of twigs and grasses nestled in the bottom. Built entirely by the female, the nest is constructed from a narrow structure of long strands hanging loosely from a branch. The bird knots smaller fibers of grasses and reeds crosswise into the framework, making the walls thicker and adding support.

The females go to such great lengths to suspend the nest solely to avoid predation. A colony's nests hang so far from the tree that camouflage is not essential. The nests wave freely like flags in the breeze, safe from all but the strongest winds.

Crested Oropendolas (Psarocolius decumanus) *possess strong, pointed, conical bills that aid them in pushing and pulling fibers into their nests. Though Crested Oropendolas are more solitary than others, they do join other oropendola flocks when nesting. Most oropendola colonies boast one dominant male and several subordinates.*

ARTISANS AT WORK

The West Indian coconut palm seems to be dripping with so much green and brown fruit that it is hard to tell which are the coconuts and which the nests. At least one hundred yellow-and-black birds are in constant motion around the small spheres that hang from nearly every branch. One bird flies in with a thin strip of grass and lands in the center of a ring of knotted vegetation. He weaves the new blade into the hoop and flies off to find more material.

It is the second nest this Village Weaver has built this season; his first was rejected by females and he had to destroy it. Now he is putting the finishing touches on his ball of grass. He has already strengthened the walls and floor of the nest and must complete an entranceway and threshold, positioned on the bottom so unwelcome visitors will have trouble entering.

After a day's work, the weaver sets out to attract a female. He clings upside down to the underside of the nest, flapping his wings and singing for attention. If his nest meets the high standards of a breeding female, she will fly in, add her own material to the inside, and mate with him. After the eggs are laid, the male weaver is free to begin another nest and repeat the whole process with a new female.

Some weavers wrap nest material around two parallel stems, which the weaver bird uses as any human weaver would a loom. Weavers are without doubt the most skillful nest builders in the avian world. They are adroit with their strong bills—able to knot, weave, and entwine grasses and other strips of vegetation with great dexterity.

Originally confined to Africa, Village Weavers (Ploceus cucullatus) also occupy islands of Hispaniola and Saona.

71

This Village Weaver begins his nest by constructing a ring of grass. From inside the ring,

he adds supporting sides and strengthens the floor. With the nest complete, the weaver hangs

from the bottom, flapping its wings to attract a female. When no females are lured by its handi-work, the weaver destroys the nest. It will begin a new nest as soon as the old one is demolished.

INHABITANTS OF MUD

Mud is an excellent choice of nesting material. When it is cemented into place, mud creates a sturdy nest that is nearly impermeable to any threat but rain, at least for the time needed to raise a family of chicks.

Cliff Swallows build their nests as do most other mud-nesters, in stages. As many as one thousand mud pellets, each carried separately to the site and placed in layers, are needed to complete the task. Before each succeeding layer can be added, the previous one must dry completely. Too much weight, and the nest could topple over.

The whole task needs about two weeks to complete and may take even longer during periods of drought or too much rain. A mud hole seems almost alive when dozens of Cliff Swallows are jockeying for the choicest mud they can find. With their wings and tails lifted high to stay clean, couples

While some ovenbirds build nests from dried vegetable matter, the Rufous Ovenbirds (Furnarius rufus) craft theirs into similarly shaped earthen vessels composed mainly of 1500 to 2500 clay pellets. All 427 species of ovenbirds live in Central or South America.

RIGHT AND OPPOSITE: *Cliff Swallows (Hirundo pyrrhonota) construct their nests in North America.*

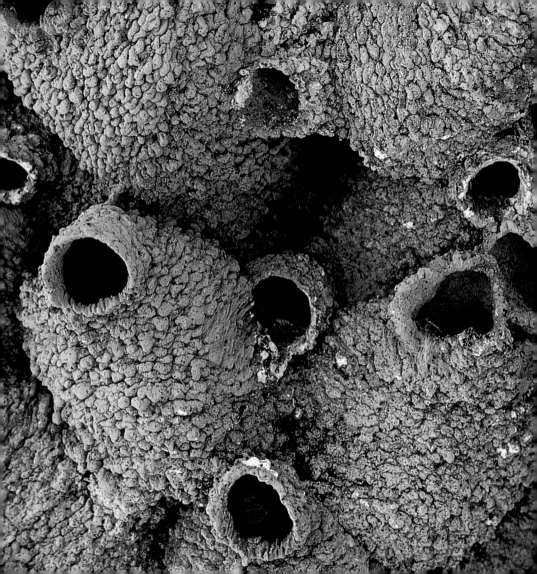

The mud in Greater Flamingo (Phoenicopterus ruber) mounds quickly hardens in the hot Bahamian sun. The depression on top of each mound cradles the flamingo's single egg.

scoop up mud and fly to a nearby cliff face. They join a colony of Cliff Swallows, whose close-fitting nests under a ledge lack defined borders and appear as one. The once smooth, rocky outcropping appears pockmarked with globular nests that look like overturned wine flasks.

Most mud nests cannot be reused in successive years without some type of patchwork—the earthen structures crumble during the interim seasons. Occasionally Cliff Swallows do not build new nests. Instead, they convert old Barn Swallow, robin, or phoebe nests by adding mud and their signature entrance tunnels.

Flamingos are among the few mud nesters that build their conical mud nests in exposed locations. A site such as the Bahamas' southernmost island, Inagua, makes an ideal spot because of its relatively light rainfall. Even so, some years whole generations of Greater Flamingos have been lost to floods.

WATERFRONT PROPERTY

ABOVE AND OPPOSITE: *Common Loons* (Gavia immer), *which live in the northern regions of North America, build their nests out of grasses, moss, or floating vegetation. When disturbed, incubating loons scamper to the water's edge, dive in, surface a distance away, and attempt to deflect attention from their nest.*

Many aquatic birds build their nests very close to or just on top of the water. Some birds, such as coots, build their own private nest islands on the water, while grebes anchor floating platforms to a nearby water plant. As long as the eggs stay dry (and out of the jaws of a predator), the unhatched chicks remain safe. Unfortunately, such proximity to water is not without risk. Water can easily damage an egg, destroying the embryo. Common Loons, which usually nest on the edge of isolated islands or peninsulas near freshwater lakes, often find their nests—and their brood—eradicated by floods.

Loons develop nests from modest scrapes to which they add material after the eggs are laid. Many birds use this technique to build a nest custom-made to fit perfectly around their bodies. Both loon parents, generally of equal size, share in the process. While one builds or incubates, the other usually avails itself of the local fish.

Though loons fish in both fresh and salt water, they nest near fresh water only. Free of the currents and tidal motion of seawater, the calmer waters of inland lakes are easier for neonates to negotiate while learning the diving techniques crucial for their adult survival.

IN A CROWD

Life on a cliff ledge can be precarious. One wrong step out of the nest could lead to a sudden death. Snuggled into a dried-out nest of seaweed and mud, a fluffy Red-legged Kittiwake chick grasps onto its nest with strong claws every time the wind blows. The cliff face on the small island in Alaska is littered with Kittiwake nests. Even though they are not directly adjacent to each other, they still benefit from the closeness.

Communal or colonial birds nest on tiny territories sometimes only a foot or two apart. About one tenth of the world's bird species nest in colonies, not because they are lonely and crave company, but because they increase their chances of survival by doing so. One of the main reasons to nest in groups is defense—a gang of birds can do more to fend off a predator than one bird acting alone. Breeding in large congregations, these birds also minimize the risk of individual attack.

Life in such tight quarters engenders its share of problems. Chief among these are aggressive birds who fight, steal eggs, filch nesting material, and even covet their neighbor's mate. Birds must be careful to guard what little property they have.

Kittiwakes nesting in such tight spaces are at a disadvantage when it comes to fighting. They cannot possibly perform aerial attacks, nor rush headlong into battle. This doesn't stop them from skirmishing—it just makes the contest more challenging. Kittiwakes duel with their bills, while keeping their bodies mostly still. Skirmishes in large communities disturb the marginal peace, and social skills are at a premium.

PRECEDING PAGES: *Red-legged Kittiwakes* (Rissa brevirostris) *nest on Alaska's Pribilof Islands and the Commander Islands off the coast of Siberia.*

LEFT: *To maximize the effectiveness of a colony, most member birds synchronize their egg-laying to within days of each other. When all birds are occupied with similar tasks, greater cooperation is ensured. Thick-billed Murres* (Uria lomvia) *breed on islands off both coasts of North America's Arctic regions, including Alaska, Greenland, Iceland, and some parts of Eurasia.*

When space is at a premium, birds restrict their territories to the size of their nests. A Great Blue Heron (Ardea herodias), *commonly found throughout the Americas, shares nesting space with Cattle Egrets* (Bubulcus ibis). *Originally from Africa but now spread throughout much of North America and the West Indies, the gregarious egrets typically nest and feed with other herons.*

HEAPS AND MOUNDS

Australia's Brush Turkeys (Alectura lathami) *build their nest mounds in the rain forests and scrubs of Queensland. Though constructed mainly of decaying vegetation, the mounds are topped by a layer of dirt that shakes loose from the feet of a building male.*

In practically every bird species, some parental care is necessary to raise chicks. Even those that hatch with fairly well developed bodies need an adult to keep them warm at night and teach them basic survival skills. The megapodes that live in the warm tropical forests of Australasia are a notable exception.

Megapodes use their large legs and feet to create the twelve-foot-wide, three-foot-high hills of fermenting vegetation that serve as nests. A breeding Brush Turkey male scrapes plant matter off the ground and flings it into a pile behind him. Every so often he stops and climbs aboard the pile, stamping it into a compact mound. The mound is constantly attended to, especially as the vegetation decomposes and ferments. The temperature in the mound can soar well above 100°F, but the male eases it down to a more manageable 95° by creating pockets and releasing excess heat.

During the building process, Brush Turkeys refuse to be interrupted or intruded upon. They are especially aggressive toward other males, but they do not welcome females either, until they are ready to mate. After mating, the female lays her eggs in the mound, burying them several inches beneath the surface, and leaves. The male continues checking and regulating the temperature of the mound to ensure proper incubation of the eggs, adding more vegetation midway to prolong the fermentation process.

Just before the chicks are born, the male disappears. Megapode chicks never get to know either parent. They are born well developed and spend their first moments clawing their way out of the earthen grave that has given them life.

Scrubfowl (Megapodius reinwardt) *are found in coastal northern Australia. In addition to rain forests and scrub areas, they sometimes nest among mangroves.*

SCENE-STEALERS

A Brown-headed Cowbird (Molothrus ater) *egg lies inside a MacGillivray's Warbler's* (Oporornis tolmiei) *nest.*

OPPOSITE: *In addition to laying eggs in another's nest, outright theft of nesting materials is a common occurrence, as demonstrated by this Magnificent Frigatebird* (Fregata magnificens) *grabbing vegetation from the mouth of a gannet in mid-flight.*

Often a bird perfectly capable of building a nest and sustaining young will lay her eggs in the nest of a fellow bird of the same species. This odd behavior may be a reaction to environmental limitations or the result of hormonal deficiencies in individual birds; they possess the instinct to lay eggs, but not to build nests. Other egg bestowers simply do not have the drive to rear their own chicks or build a nest. Called brood parasites, these species depend on the kindness of strangers for survival.

Brood parasites do not have it easy, especially since they must constantly be sneaking into another bird's territory. Hens wait until a target nest is left unprotected, lay their eggs quickly, and fly away, leaving no trace of their trespass save the alien egg.

Brood parasites must be somewhat particular as to whom to entrust with their eggs—choosing foster families with similar food, incubation, and fledging needs as their chicks'. Cowbirds are not as fussy as cuckoos, whydahs, and honey guides, who look for species that lay eggs of similar size and color. Instead, they rely on numbers being in their favor—depositing their eggs in countless sparrow, warbler, finch, flycatcher, and vireo nests, even though the difference in the appearance of the eggs can be extreme. Often, the host bird will discover the ruse and dispatch the unhatched chicks to a merciless death or abandon them, along with its own progeny. In a few hapless cases, a host adult, recognizing a foreign element in the nest, mistakenly tosses out its own egg and hatches the interloper instead.

UNUSUAL SITES

Habitat destruction has caused the disappearance of countless animal species worldwide. Most simply cannot adapt to the loss of their living space and so die from lack of appropriate food or shelter. Some do not reproduce, and their generational line eventually dies out. They cannot compete with the onslaught of civilization.

Some birds, however, have managed to cope with development and even thrived. In some cases, their adaptability has not only saved them, but helped to increase their numbers. After their introduction to North America in the 1890s, European Starlings took over nesting cavities of indigenous birds, often kicking out the original occupants.

European Starlings are not fussy birds. Their nests are routinely found in noisy airports, high-rise apartment buildings, bridge girders, and backyard trees. They are also appreciative of a well-built nest box, though hobbyists trying to attract swallows, bluebirds, or wrens may not return the sentiment.

Any bird able to adapt to unusual circumstances in the absence of preferred nesting habitats has a greater chance of long-term survival. Such locations as telephone poles, fence posts, building ledges, chimneys, and rooftops have all become the adopted homes of different birds. Names such as Chimney Swift, Barn Owl, House Finch, and House Sparrow reflect a preference for man-made structures. Unorthodox nesting areas must still satisfy the basic requirements of safety from predators, proximity to food source, and security for the eggs.

The European Starling (Sturnus vulgaris) *is found throughout North American cities, suburbs, woodlands, and agricultural areas. The hundred birds introduced from Europe into New York City's Central Park in the 1890s have increased to at least a million.*

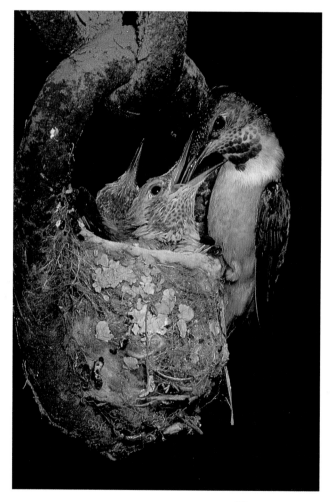

LEFT: *Unexpected locations, such as large industrial chains, are excellent hiding places for nests. Only the smallest of birds, such as this Allen's Hummingbird* (Selasphorus sasin), *found in Pacific coast parks and woods, could make use of such tiny quarters.*

OPPOSITE: *Many birds, such as the Canada Goose* (Branta canadensis), *have no problem adapting to artificial nest sites, even though they may not be as pleasing to the eye as a tree or waterfront property.*

MASTER BUILDERS

BELOW AND OPPOSITE:
*Africa's Hamerkops
(Scopus umbretta),
sometimes also called
Hammerheads, build
their mansions in strong
trees along watercourses
and marshlands. Pairs
typically mate on the
roof of their nests.*

While weavers may boast the most skilled builders, Hamerkops possess the greatest endurance, and build by far the most elaborate and complex nests. For sheer size, Hamerkop nests rival raptors' aeries. But unlike the haphazard construction of the raptors, a Hamerkop pair puts quite a bit of method and design into building their home.

Made of at least eight thousand twigs and branches cemented together with mud and dung, the nest has the look of a rudimentary tree house. Hamerkops build the sides and back first, and then fabricate a strong roof, almost three feet thick, on the top. Inside, the nest is divided into an entranceway and separate chambers. The avian homeowners add constantly to the nest, even after their eggs hatch.

Most native observers don't believe a 6½-foot-high and three- to six-foot-wide nest, weighing over five hundred pounds, could be built by just one pair of birds. In fact, one couple does all the building, though it may take as long as six months to complete the work. A Xhosa tribal legend holds that the residents use one room for eating, one for nesting, and one for spending the day. Though people leave them alone, even after the Hamerkops have abandoned them, other birds and creatures of the savannah are known to take up residence in a Hamerkop villa once the original owners have vacated the premises.

MAKING DO WITH NOTHING

ABOVE AND OPPOSITE:
*The White or Fairy
Tern* (Gygis alba) *lives
throughout tropical and
subtropical oceans, espe-
cially near the equator.*

A cozy, well-hidden nest is the most effective protection a parent can provide its egg. For birds who choose remote islands as
nesting grounds, however, the pressure to put up defenses is
considerably less. These inaccessible spots can be reached only
by air, and are therefore free from typical mainland predators
such as mongooses and snakes. When predators are not a problem, birds are freer in their nesting choices. Eggs can be laid in
plain sight, with little fear of danger. Shorebirds typically put
the least amount of energy into their nests. Most make only a
scrape, and a few, no nest at all.

One of the most unusual nonnesters is the White or Fairy
Tern. Unlike other terns, it nests alone, and unlike nearly
every other bird, it lays its single egg, unprotected and uncon-
cealed, on the branch of a tree or on the ledge of a cliff or
rock. It prefers trees, particularly casuarinas, which have many
bumps and knots on their branches. The small egg rests in the
fork of a tree or abuts one of the many knots, and that is all the
security provided. The parents, in a remarkable display of balance and grace, incubate the egg for five weeks on the branch.
Astonishingly few eggs crack when they are laid or fall to the
ground during incubation.

The single Fairy Tern chick must learn to balance immediately after breaking through its shell and is happily gifted with
strong feet and claws to assist it in its task. The chick instinc-
tively grabs the branch so tightly that it rarely falls off, but
often finds itself swept upside down by prevailing winds.

ABOVE AND OPPOSITE TOP: *Both the Yellow-wattled* (Vanellus malabaricus) *and the Red-wattled Lapwing* (Vanellus indicus) *of Asia lay their solitary eggs on bare ground.*

LEFT: *Often a single egg, such as that of the Thick-billed Murre* (Uria lomvia), *is laid not on cushiony sand, but on bare rock.*

OPPOSITE BOTTOM: *When the terrain is too rough for a scrape, an Arctic Tern* (Sterna paradisaea) *lays her eggs among the rocks and shells.*

PART THREE

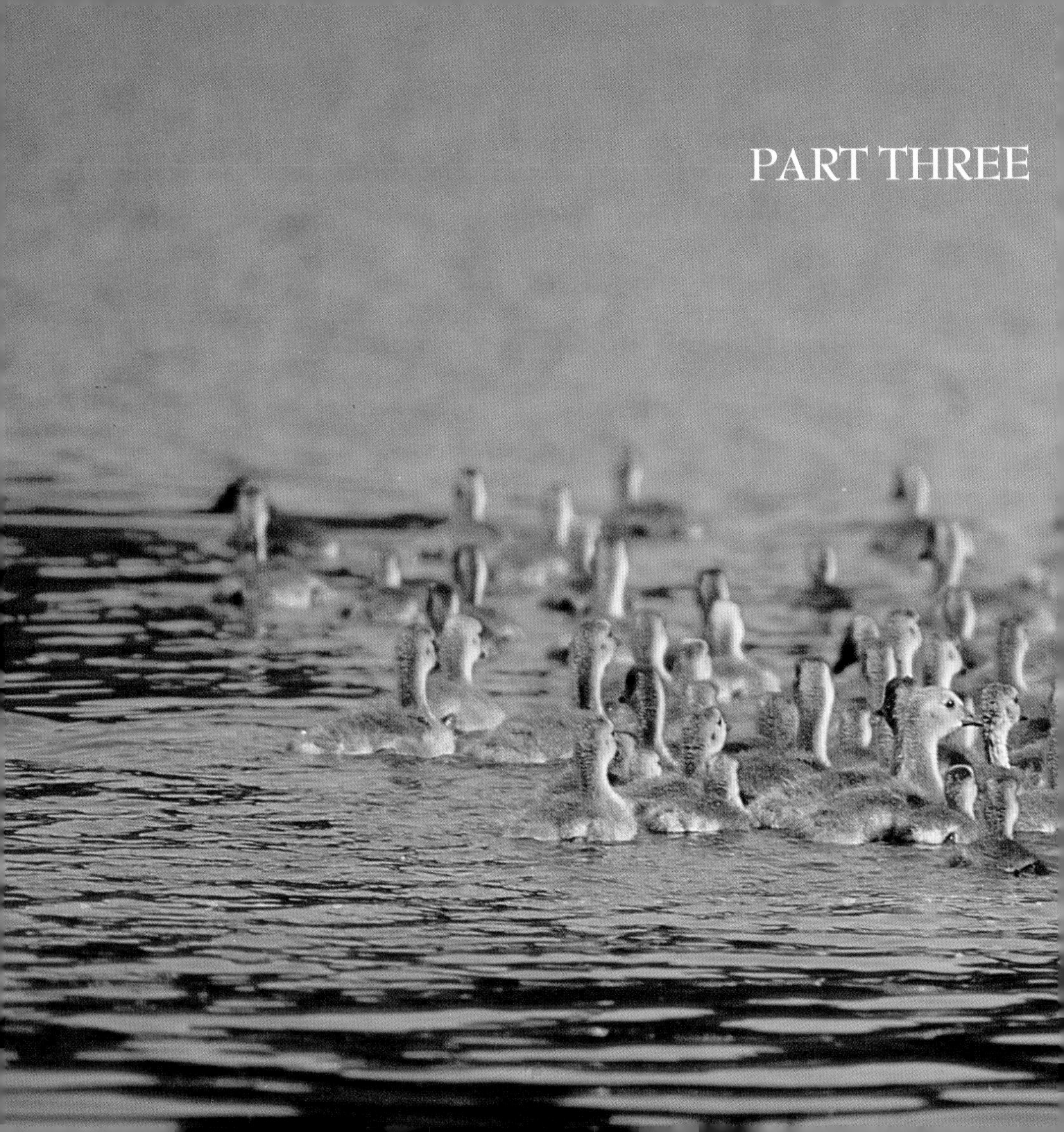

In the Nest and Out

A nest is not truly tested until after the eggs are laid. The structure must be able to withstand the rigors of foul weather, the weight of the eggs, and in many instances, the activities of growing chicks.

In most cases, shortly after the nest is complete or acquired, the female deposits the first egg. Most eggs are laid at the first light of day, when energy levels are at their highest. With some exceptions, they arrive one at a time, every other day. Often the first egg a female ever lays in her life is sterile, with no yolk inside. In later broods, the chick that emerges from the first egg is not always the strongest and is often outranked by the occupant of the second.

Usually, the clutch size correlates with the type of chick. Altricial birds, whose chicks require extended care by one or both parents, tend to have small clutches and tinier eggs, making it easier to feed their

PRECEDING PAGES: *Several families of Canada Geese* (Branta canadensis) *herd their youngsters into a* crèche *or gosling nursery.*

LEFT: *A Herring Gull* (Larus argentatus) *pecks its way out of its shell.*

OPPOSITE: *Cattle Egret chicks* (Bulbulcus ibis) *usually fledge after twenty-five days in the nest.*

charges. Precocial chicks, on the other hand, which can at least partially care for themselves after birth, tend to be part of big broods and hatch from larger eggs.

The brooding parent must do more than maintain the proper temperature for incubation. They must turn the eggs regularly until shortly before they hatch to prevent their contents from adhering to the shell. Before hatching time, the parents become much more attached to their eggs and less likely to abandon them when alarmed.

Most chicks use a temporary egg tooth, which they lose upon hatching, to chisel their way out of the egg. The first days of life for an altricial chick can be a constant battle.

The newly hatched chick may be subject to starvation or attack from its brothers and sisters. Some adults even eat their weaker young. Each time they return to the nest, roadrunner parents inspect their chicks; those that are too fragile or lethargic are tossed into the air and swallowed whole.

If they make it through their first days, chicks spend most of their early energies eating and sleeping, but they must soon turn their attention to flying and finding their own food. After some fledglings such as swallows, robins, and grosbeaks master flight, they still need their parents for food. These skills can sometimes take days, weeks, or months to perfect.

BORN HELPLESS

After over three long weeks of incubation, a Barn Owl chick pokes its way out of its shell. There's been much commotion outside the egg's tiny confines, though it hasn't been rolled onto its side in days. After a few hours of concentrated pecking, the chick finds itself on a soft pile of hay. It has no idea it is in the rafters of a country barn nor does it see its larger sisters, brothers, or parents. Born blind and without much downy covering, all it can do is lie still and cry for the food and warmth it craves.

Altricial young are born completely dependent on their parents for nourishment, safety, and even warmth. The chicks remain in the nest until they are strong enough to fend for themselves. The nest need not be a highly structured one, such as a cup or enclosed nest, but a secure nest, out of reach of predators, is essential.

Most altricial chicks grow quickly, since they expend little energy seeking food and may even grow larger than their parents. Colorfully gaping mouths signal the chicks' hunger. Many chicks have target areas—ridges lining their open mouths—which aid in food placement. Encouraging altricial young to abandon this cozy existence can take some coaxing on the part of parents. Many simply stop feeding their young, allowing hunger to persuade the chicks most eloquently. Until they get the point and leave, chicks live off their fat reserves.

Barn Owls (Tyto alba) *are found in tropical and temperate locations on most continents except in mountainous coniferous forests.*

LEFT: *This Magnificent Frigatebird chick* (Fregata magnificens), *like most altricial young, is born without insulating feathers. Unable to regulate their body temperature, they require the heat from their parents to survive the cooler tropical evenings.*

OPPOSITE: *Living chiefly in northern Eurasia and northern North America, Cedar Waxwings* (Bombycilla cedrorum) *often lay two broods in the same season. Females may resume courtship behavior when their first brood is just seven days old.*

READY FOR ACTION

Unlike their more helpless brethren, precocial chicks require little parental assistance. Born with a covering of down and the ability to see, most are able to care for themselves almost immediately after hatching.

Precocial birds usually lay their eggs on or near the ground. Waterfowl and waders almost always nest near water —their immediate source of food and sustenance. Accompanied by their mother, these chicks scamper toward the water almost as soon as they emerge from the egg. In later forays, family groups combine, though mothers and chicks remain ever aware of each other's presence.

Bonding is crucial to the precocial chicks' survival, and the relationship between chick and mother begins even before it is hatched. In the later stages of development unhatched chicks begin calling from inside the egg. The unhatched chicks even communicate among themselves and it is thought that through these exchanges they help coordinate their hatching to within hours of each other.

Precocial hens can lay larger clutches than altricial birds because most precocial chicks quickly learn to feed themselves. A typical Blue-winged Teal lays her clutch of ten to twelve eggs at the rate of one every one or two days but they are not incubated until the last is in the nest. Soon after they are hatched, the mother teal escorts her brown-and-yellow downy chicks to the water for their first swim.

Blue-winged Teal chicks (Anas discors) *huddle together for warmth. They are found in North, Central, and northern South America.*

Common Loons (Gavia immer) *are considered semiprecocial. Although they can leave the nest shortly after hatching, they still depend on their parents for food since they must be taught to dive. They shelter on the adults' backs for the first few weeks of their lives.*

Not yet equipped with water-repellent feathers, American Coot chicks (Fulica americana) *are particularly vulnerable to rain. When dry, this North American native boasts the fluffy down characteristic of semiprecocial chicks, as well as a set of well-developed legs that enable it to leave the nest soon after breaking through its shell. Unlike many other semiprecocial birds, coots may hatch as much as twenty-four hours apart.*

CHANGELINGS

A Brown-headed Cowbird chick (Molothrus ater) far outweighs its Wood Pewee nest mates.

Once a brood parasite has managed to slip her egg into a host's nest, her reproductive role is essentially over. She leaves each chick to fend for itself, in a family that did not choose to raise it. There's no reason to feel sorry for the uninvited foster chick, however; it is the unwitting adoptive parents that might soon face an unexpected brutality—the ruthless slaying of all their own offspring.

Many brood parasites, such as cuckoos, immediately dispatch of their nest mates as soon as they hatch by summarily tossing them over the side of the nest. African Honeyguides use far deadlier methods to eliminate their fellows. Equipped from birth with hooks at the tips of their mandibles, they efficiently wield these needle-sharp barbs against defenseless nest mates.

Cowbirds do not employ such direct methods, yet they just as effectively eliminate the competition. Their companions often die of starvation because the larger, more aggressive cowbird grabs all the food. It is a wonder that the adults still feed the chick when they realize the disparity in size. Yet in most cases, the adults accept it, even if it appears double the size of its foster parent and requires twice the care of its siblings.

Not all brood parasites oust their nest mates. Parents of the whydah family choose species that closely resemble them, such as waxbills. Not only do the eggs match in coloration, but the chicks resemble their hosts as well. They even have the same markings in their gaping mouths which signal hunger to an observing adult. Whydahs blend in with their adopted families instead of destroying them.

A Brown-headed Cowbird chick needs only a short incubation and grows quickly in its first days of life. The advantage it gains helps it appropriate most of the food and easily over-whelm its foster siblings.

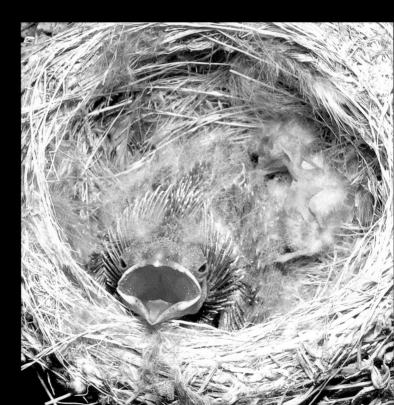

IN DEFENSE OF THE NEST

A Least Grebe (Podiceps dominicus) *surprises a snake attempting to steal its egg.*

Grebes are extremely protective of their young. When newly hatched, chicks ride piggyback and submerge beneath the water with their parents when they are alarmed. A grebe egg, laid in thick marshes or inland lakes, is vulnerable to attack from many predators, especially sly snakes, which threaten unannounced visits.

Birds are at their most vulnerable during the nesting season. Most can do little to protect their eggs once discovered. Some put up brave fights or feign injury to lure a predator away. Ducks and geese routinely cover their nests with down when they have to leave it unwatched. After the chicks are hatched, altricial parents typically remove shells to a location far from the nest. Broken eggshells are a telltale sign that new life, and therefore a scrumptious meal, awaits an alert hunter.

Some enemies are not as obvious as a snake or carnivorous mammal. A common nest nuisance, bluebottle fly larvae feed on nestling blood. Many birds try to nest as early in the season as possible to avoid these and other disease-carrying insects. Red-breasted Nuthatches employ imaginative means to battle insect pests, such as applying sticky fly-catching substances to the outsides of their entrance holes.

Several birds have adopted uncanny methods of thwarting potential predators. When enemies approach, Burrowing Owls make rasping noises like a rattlesnake from inside their dens. To complete the picture, they sometimes leave discarded snake skins at the entrance. Despite the best precautions, however, luck and circumstance often afford the best protection.

Camouflage is the best defense against unwanted intruders. North America's Sandhill Crane (Grus canadensis) lies low, covers its entire nest with its body, and uses its neutral coloration to blend in with its surroundings.

When a Crowned Plover (Vanellus coronatus) of eastern or southern Africa believes its nest is threatened, it sometimes feigns a broken wing to lure a predator away from its young. After the plover uses this device to fool its enemy, it takes flight, escaping danger at the last moment.

Few predators inhabit the Antarctic peninsula where Imperial Shags (Phalacrocorax atriceps) *lay their eggs in enormous colonies, but that doesn't mean the parent can be any less vigilant. Even the most innocent intruder receives a warning to keep away.*

When Western Gull (Larus occidentalis) *parents are concerned about their wandering chicks, they sound alarm calls. The youngsters respond by scampering to a secure area and crouching down.*

AGAINST
THE ELEMENTS

Even a well-built, well-situated nest can succumb to the vagaries of unexpectedly foul weather. Strong winds knock structures out of trees and teeming rain easily decomposes mud nests. A bird can do little to combat a sudden downpour but wait it out and hope for the best. Often breeding must be postponed until the following season.

In areas of predictably extreme weather conditions, birds have devised elaborate coping strategies. Birds nesting in scorchingly hot habitats lie flat on their eggs to absorb the heat, spreading their wings to avoid overheating themselves. Those that nest near water sources avail themselves of this natural coolant, wetting their breast feathers and transferring moisture to the eggs or dripping water from their mouths into the nest.

At the opposite extreme, temperatures in Antarctica are high enough for breeding for only a few months. Instead of racing the clock, King Penguins lengthen their breeding cycle by taking time out for the cold. King Penguins lay their eggs either in November and December or February and March. During incubation the egg rests on the adult's feet, warmed by a fold in the parent's skin. Fed by both adults, the overly fattened chick reaches only partial maturity. Its size depends on how late in the breeding season it hatched. Most survive quite well by staying huddled together, living off their fat reserves. Growth does not resume until the following spring when both the food supply and the weather are more inviting.

PRECEDING PAGES:
King Penguins
(Aptenodytes patago-
nicus) *are found on sub-
Antarctic islands and
neighboring seas.*

OPPOSITE AND RIGHT:
Imperial Shags (Phala-
crocorax atriceps), *a
type of cormorant, regu-
larly nest in colonies with
penguins and albatrosses.
Since Imperial Shags live
on the Antarctic Penin-
sula, they face many of
the same problems as
penguins. Even in the
Antarctic summer, cold
and snow are regular
concerns. If egg tempera-
tures cannot be regulated,
developing embryos do
not survive.*

Scarlet Macaw of South America

EPILOGUE

Today millions of birds struggle to survive in a world increasingly inhospitable to their needs. One of the greatest controllers of population expansion among birds is the decreasing availability of nesting areas. Some birds, such as sparrows, are highly adaptable, as evidenced by their success in adjusting to the encumbrances of urban life. Others have suffered dramatic losses in population—even to the brink of extinction—all because their specific needs are simply not being met. Natural disasters are an expected part of life for birds; their populations ebb and flow with dry and wet seasons, forest fires, earthquakes, and volcanic eruptions. Yet nowhere in nature were birds prepared for the large-

Nankeen Kestrels (Falco cenchroides) *have avoided extinction—adapting to city buildings, railyards, and farms when it is not possible to nest on cliffs or plains.*

scale, human-instigated devastation to nesting areas that has decimated many formerly thriving avian communities.

Thousands of choice nesting sites have been mowed down in the name of progress—trees felled and converted to timber, or even discarded, though their cavities may be filled with nesting mergansers, Wood Ducks, owls, kestrels, and songbirds. It isn't only the nest site that is at risk. Once drained or paved, rest stops along popular migration routes, such as wetlands and inland waterways, are no longer available. Without these respites, birds traveling north or south to their nesting areas never make it to their appointed destinations to build their nests.

Not all human contribution to the decline of nesting sites has been as deliberate. The "innocent" introduction of the European Starling to Central Park over a hundred years ago resulted in one of the most disastrous population explosions in North American bird history. The now millionfold population, sighted in virtually every state in the union, has usurped the nesting areas of countless birds and contributed to the decline of several other species.

Birds that cannot find a place to nest simply don't reproduce. There are no picket lines of protest, no organized aggression toward those who encroach on their territory. They live their lives and die, as usual, without leaving descendants. The only hint of their plight is their absence.

Humans occasionally rise to the challenge of protecting birds and assisting them to survive. In 1957, the Michigan Department of Natural Resources set aside state forest lands for the protection of the Kirtland's Warbler, a bird with very particular nesting requirements. A single nesting pair requires at least thirty acres of Jack Pines, eight to twenty years old, found solely in Michigan's lower northern peninsula. Since there are few tracts in the area with eighty or more acres, much land had to be set aside to ensure their survival. The Kirtland's Warbler will nest nowhere else in the world.

It is the exception rather than the rule for a bird species to be granted such strict protection. Limited government intervention has aided some birds, such as the Spotted Owl, nearly forced to extinction by the loss of their habitat.

Each Spotted Owl (Strix occidentalis) *pair requires hundreds of acres of territory for nesting.*

Unfortunately, many loggers have reacted by transferring their anger and frustration onto a defenseless species, viewing the effort to ensure the bird's survival as a threat to the livelihood of thousands of human beings. Both sides of this issue cite bird nests as the center of the controversy: as a *cause célèbre* for the environmentalists who fight to preserve the nesting grounds, and as a convenient scapegoat for loggers frustrated in their attempts to cut down the ancient trees and make a living in hard economic times.

Habitat preservation is one way people can help birds to survive, while providing a nest substitute may be another possibility. Nesting platforms in the Chesapeake Bay area directly contribute to the survival of the Osprey in that region and the continued presence of Purple Martins in North America can be attributed to the multiple-dwelling bird condominiums that have all but replaced the martin's nesting habitat. What once began as a hobby has become the only hope of survival for quite a few bird species.

Ospreys (Pandion haliaetus) *almost became extinct in the 1960s when DDT contaminated their fish supply.*

It is difficult to convince a person with a mortgage and bills to pay that a bird's future counts for more than his or her paycheck. Since no money in the world can replace an extinct species, when is the right time to take action? Would a world without a warbler singing, a weaver weaving, a crane dancing, or a tiny hummingbird nesting in its even tinier nest, be a world we'd want to live in?

INDEX

ACKNOWLEDGMENTS

There have been countless individuals who have assisted me in the writing of this book, either through moral support, metaphoric consultations, or tedious reads and rereads of my work. Special thanks are due to Linda Manoogian, Janeil Engelstad, Diane Greenfeld, Ann Guilfoyle, Martin Harvey, Mark Barton, Noah Scalin, Nan Wise, and my mother, Lucille Kupietz. —*Sharon A. Cohen*

PHOTOGRAPHIC CREDITS

The photographs in *Bird Nests* were provided by Gerry Ellis and are copyright © Gerry Ellis except as noted below.

Courtesy of The Wildlife Collection: © Gary Bell, pp. 37 (top), 48; © Michael Francis, p. 32; © D. Robert Franz, pp. 12, 20, 33, 34, 35 (top and bottom), 57 (left), 63 (bottom); © Martin Harvey, pp. 14, 50–51, 72 (left and right), 73 (left and right), 92, 93; © Henry Holdsworth, pp. 17, 62, 74 (bottom), 116 (top); © Tim Laman, p. 16; © Robert Lankinen, pp. 7, 22, 23, 26 (top), 54–55, 59, 66, 78, 79, 91, 100, 105, 108; © Vivek R. Sinha, pp. 8, 96 (top), 97 (top); © Jack Swenson, pp. 27, 28–29, 82, 87. Courtesy of Tom Stack & Associates: © Mary Clay, pp. 112, 113; © Jeff Foott, pp. 86, 111. Courtesy of VIREO: © C. A. Fogle, p. 90; © Gary Nuechterlein, pp. 38–39. Individual Credits: © Thomas C. Boyden, pp. 49 (top and bottom), 69, 74 (top), 83, 117 (bottom); © David Cavagnaro, pp. 94, 95; © Rob Curtis, pp. 68, 115; © Michael Durham, jacket flap (bottom); © Janeil Engelstad, jacket flap (top); © Eugene Schulz, pp. 53 (top and bottom), 118–119.

ACKNOWLEDGMENTS

There have been countless individuals who have assisted me in the writing of this book, either through moral support, metaphoric consultations, or tedious reads and rereads of my work. Special thanks are due to Linda Manoogian, Janeil Engelstad, Diane Greenfeld, Ann Guilfoyle, Martin Harvey, Mark Barton, Noah Scalin, Nan Wise, and my mother, Lucille Kupietz. —*Sharon A. Cohen*

PHOTOGRAPHIC CREDITS

The photographs in *Bird Nests* were provided by Gerry Ellis and are copyright © Gerry Ellis except as noted below.

Courtesy of The Wildlife Collection: © Gary Bell, pp. 37 (top), 48; © Michael Francis, p. 32; © D. Robert Franz, pp. 12, 20, 33, 34, 35 (top and bottom), 57 (left), 63 (bottom); © Martin Harvey, pp. 14, 50–51, 72 (left and right), 73 (left and right), 92, 93; © Henry Holdsworth, pp. 17, 62, 74 (bottom), 116 (top); © Tim Laman, p. 16; © Robert Lankinen, pp. 7, 22, 23, 26 (top), 54–55, 59, 66, 78, 79, 91, 100, 105, 108; © Vivek R. Sinha, pp. 8, 96 (top), 97 (top); © Jack Swenson, pp. 27, 28–29, 82, 87. Courtesy of Tom Stack & Associates: © Mary Clay, pp. 112, 113; © Jeff Foott, pp. 86, 111. Courtesy of VIREO: © C. A. Fogle, p. 90; © Gary Nuechterlein, pp. 38–39. Individual Credits: © Thomas C. Boyden, pp. 49 (top and bottom), 69, 74 (top), 83, 117 (bottom); © David Cavagnaro, pp. 94, 95; © Rob Curtis, pp. 68, 115; © Michael Durham, jacket flap (bottom); © Janeil Engelstad, jacket flap (top); © Eugene Schulz, pp. 53 (top and bottom), 118–119.